Heart Murmur

Emma Storr

*Calder Valley
Poetry*

Published 2019 by Calder Valley Poetry
www.caldervalleypoetry.com
caldervalleypoetry@yahoo.com

ISBN 978-1-9997062-9-6

Designed and typeset in Garamond by Bob Horne

Printed by Amadeus Press, Ezra House, West 26 Business Park,
Cleckheaton, West Yorkshire, BD19 4TQ.
www.amadeuspress.co.uk

Contents

For Paul, Catherine and Stephen with much love.

Differential

He offers a mangled tube of ointment,
name half-obscured on the underbelly.
He needs it for those recurring spots.
He says it's nothing serious,
he's had it before,
but it seems to be spreading.
No, he doesn't want me to look.

She has 'saved it all up' for me.
She flourishes a list on lined paper
clutched in her pebbled hand,
ticks off each item as if
this guaranteed a cure.
She mentions, as she gets dressed,
that new ache she's noticed.
It keeps her awake.
She hopes it's nothing serious,
the beginning of an invasion
we can't stop.

The baby is hot and fretful.
She can't tell me what's wrong:
a screech unlike her usual cry;
an odour of ill health.
No signs of anything serious
but I spread out my safety net,
check there are no holes
where a little one could slip through.

I weigh the evidence,
invisible scales tipping
towards the obvious.
I pray I'm not blind to red flags
waving in the wind.
I hope I'm not missing
the unicorn that is waiting,
waiting.

Eye to Eye

I'm in your face
searchlight in hand, peering
through your window.
I scan for the concave
dew pond, look for snakes
emerging from its centre,
glistening, complete.

Your shutter falls.
I step back.

Please look at where the wall and ceiling meet.
Keep staring. Don't move.

I steady you,
and myself,
hand on shoulder,
hold my breath.
I check there are
no cotton wool wisps,
no bursts of flames,
flares of alarm.

Your shutter falls.
I step back.

Nearly done. Look at the picture on the wall.
Yes, that one. Keep still.

I shine the beam
towards, away.
The frame narrows,
widens. I see
the safety sign of
synchronized
black holes.

You leave, I type,
all boxes filled
apart from one.
The colour of your eyes.

Delivery

Beached on the bed, squeezed by pain,
I felt them surge, then change their minds.

One heartbeat slowed, slid downhill.
Worried voices overhead.

Needles in my back, my arm,
robes of green draped my view.

Anointed, framed, my body theirs,
the scalpel cut a straight line.

They pulled each baby out fast,
as if they might drown each other.

Midnight slipped between their births,
the witching hour split in two.

Routine Appointment

She took off half her face
before we started,
placed it on the desk
in front of us.

There was the glass eye,
the moulded cheek,
the scaffold of a jaw,
shining teeth.

I thought of those plastic
models, muscle layers
unclipped from bone,
we'd studied for exams.

So different from the woman
opposite me, who
opened up a cavern
inside her warm head.

Gazing into the gap
I found nothing except
my own repulsion,
veiled with fascination.

I spoke to her worried stare,
said all seemed well,
tried to treat her
as intact, complete,

not as a damaged bowl
that might leak blood
or tears over me when
I asked her how she felt.

Six-week Check

I wake you. Unpeel your clothes
to hold you naked in my hands.
You look surprised at being new.

I murmur nonsense while I note
your symmetry and serious gaze,
the texture, tone and feel of you.

Your brain is heavy, busy growing
like a walnut in its shell.
Your fontanelles are soft to touch.

I auscultate your rapid heart,
impatient, tapping at your ribs.
You startle in expected ways,

fling your arms, reflexes brisk.
You turn to noise. Each orifice
is present, patent, hard at work.

I hand you back to anxious arms,
catch your baked cub-like scent.
I circle 'normal' on my list.

You yawn and fall back into dreams,
unaware you've passed my tests.
We won't need to meet again.

Clinical Trials

When I fed our relationship
into the analysis pipeline
the emerging data showed:
wild-type spermatocytes
oscillating in phases of
excitation and inhibition
with a standard deviation
of $Y(h-m)$, you bastard.

Our multivariate algorithm
had zero-lag correlations
and might have worked
but your spatial leakage
and lack of control meant
our coupling strength
dwindled. No stable
steady state, you bastard.

I have moved on.
What interests me now
is researching potential
enhancers of synchrony.
I hear you are using
an orthogonal model
to activate, conjugate
and most likely ligate,
you bastard.

Acknowledgements

You did not have ethics approval.
Your control group was out of control.
Your random sampling was not so bloody random.

You bastard.

Heart Murmur

My heart doesn't have to think.
It works on impulse: squeeze, relax.

It speeds up when I climb hills,
slow dances during sleep

until it's hijacked, slewed by lust,
the chemicals of longing

swirling through its chambers.
Then it aches and clambers out

raw muscle stuck to my sleeve.
It risks snagging on a nail

or attracting a hungry dog.
I am scared. It palpitates.

I stuff it back behind my ribs,
give up on men, again, again.

Doctor Jekyll Goes to Work

M & S shirts, navy trousers,
no tie in case bacteria climb
into the knot.
Foundation of caring expression,
blusher to highlight those
anxious cheekbones,
a smudge of eye shadow
to deepen the bags, heavy
with the worry of patients.

A considered lapse
each day: odd socks,
small cut from shaving,
shirt tail waving goodbye
on the ward. Everyone
can see that he hasn't time
to look after himself.

At home, at night,
his face disappears with
wet wipes. He takes off
the smart-casual uniform,
lies on the couch, naked,
staring at the ceiling stain.
He reaches for the novel.

He knows Mr Hyde
intimately. Much better
than any of his patients.

Missed

I'm a bad doctor, failed to listen.
You died six months later.
I didn't think when you told me
you had bloating, pains in your belly.

You died six months later.
You looked so well, so alive.
You had bloating. Pains in your belly.
I said it was probably indigestion.

You looked so well. So alive.
I prescribed you medicine.
We agreed, it was probably indigestion.
The scan shocked us both.

I prescribed you medicine.
I didn't think when you told me.
The scan shocked us both.
I am a bad doctor. I failed you.

Body Parts

I

We have never seen
eye to eye so why should we
share reading glasses?

II

Liver, forgive me.
You work overtime. Should I
reward you with wine?

III

Dear Uterus, thanks
for your carefully crumpled
gifts: I love all three.

IV

My knees talk and creak,
grumble their opinions.
Bag ladies that bump.

V

I could sail away
on my feet: naviculars
steering all ten toes.

Exclusive Opportunity

Before we start, please
wipe your boots on my tongue.
Don't trip on my teeth as you step
inside. Admire the glistening
inner walls, my soft palate,
my quivering uvula.

Don't obstruct my airway!
Come this way down my gullet.
Allow the peristaltic waves
to waft you into my stomach,
sloshing with muesli, acid,
and cappuccino.

Take my hand while we surf
into my duodenum and on to
the small bowel. Note the
waterfall feature from the bile
duct, guaranteed to enhance
the fast transit of fat.

Feel free to touch my gut's
villous lining, fetal fingers
stretching out into
the river of food flowing past.
Be careful of the current,
the possible flash floods.

My terminal ileum is not
a cul-de-sac, so turn here,
and follow me to my colon,
a coiled corridor for useful
storage. Please excuse
any blasts of fetid wind,

I've had a slight problem
with the air conditioning.
Let's hurry on through mud
and slurry to the roomy rectum.
What's that? The noise of distant
dripping is not a leak.

I've been double-glazed,
insulated and plumbed
to BSI standards.

You can hear the soothing
plink of urine reaching
the bladder and distant
borborygmi – gurgles
that show my gut
has no blockages.

We are nearly at the end.
This spacious chamber has
the added charm of evacuation
on most days, so you can
re-arrange the furnishings
regularly. Keep up to date.

Thanks so much for coming.
Don't hesitate to get in touch
if you want another viewing.

Don't wait too long.
I'm expecting to be
under offer very soon.

Knotted

I am tethered to myself
and the rope is getting shorter.

Someone has tied a clove hitch
in my shoulder,
a knot to secure a mooring,
tightening as it pulls taut.
They have sprinkled grit
into the joint.
I can hear it grating
as I raise my arm,
or stretch out, unthinking,
past the crunch of gravel.

I tried a shrug
but it came out lopsided.
I have to remember
right sleeve first,
a reversal of habit.
No overhead manoeuvres.
No reaching behind with the towel.

I wonder who meshed
these tissues tight?
I want to be released
from the tangled sinews,
cleaned and oiled,
so I don't grimace or cry out
when I lift a cup,
unhook my coat.

Last night I saluted the moon
and winced.
The sky shuddered,
stars blinked.

Gaps

Sometimes connection
                              fails
you let go   of   the   thread
or   wander   off
as if another colour caught you
                              tangled
in its weft.
Numbers confuse. Frac-
                              tions make no sense.
Long   long   division
(a challenge you enjoyed)
is a chasm where you

fall
    (undetected).
You crumple the page in the newspaper
Sudoku and cross words
                              printed to tease.

Never good at navigation
          your East and West
swing   round.
The sun shifts, familiar paths
      deviate.
Home hides round corners.
Landmarks you trusted
                                        drift.

Prayer

Let me not lose who I am
Let me not fail slowly
Let me not fall and shatter
Let me not spill or leak

Let me not fail slowly
Let me not slur words
Let me not spill or leak
Let me hear no lies

Let me not slur words
Let sleep wrap me tight
Let me hear no lies
Let my body decide

Let sleep wrap me tight
Let pain wander away
Let my body decide
Let silence hold me still

Let pain wander away
Let me not fall and shatter
Let silence hold me still
Let me not lose who I was

Your Skin

holds you intact
                renews as it sloughs
                                cells to dust.
Translucent at birth
                  it thickened and stretched
                                was polished
by hormones.
              It flushed with pleasure
                        shivered when
winter's fingers
                stroked your arm
                        made your fur rise.

History is seared
              in its layers
                    the half-moon burn
the white tracks of
              your babies' escape
                        that burst appendix.

Weathered and creased
                by each bend of sunlight
                            now you tear
like tissue paper.
              Spots and raisins
                    stipple your neck.
You notice the slack
              lack of elasticity
                    in your suit
well-worn and thin
              bespoke
                shrugging off your frame.

Arion Distinctus

An emergency, she decided,
arriving white-faced at the surgery,
chains jangling on her leather jacket,
the bottle in her hand.

I confirmed it had drowned,
drowned in milk, a black
jelly sweet of a slug.
Deceased.

The Environmental Officer
was brusque: no known risks.
Best to let the dairy know.

The postman had slid on a fat one
on the paved path.
No bones broken, only
sliced skin over his shin,
a bruised hip,
an embarrassed smile.

I wonder what this small, hatless
hermaphrodite plans next,
slithering through my patients' lives
with only mucus for protection,
its gleam of destruction.

Sick Note

You can't maintain altitude.
When you swoop you swerve left.
Fluttering is difficult to sustain. You flail.
Your feathers are dry, slough when you plummet.

You stand tipped,
as if leaning on an invisible staff.
I see a frown travel across your face.
Your spine is an 'S', unwilling to straighten or flex.

My hands find muscles
like iron cables, clamped to both scapulae.
You flinch when I test your range of movement.
You can't abduct, extend or flap. Your knees quiver.

I recommend massage,
heat and nectar rubbed in daily,
ambrosia and ibuprofen with your meals.
Stretch your wings hourly to embrace the sky.

But don't fly. Don't fly.

Ovarian Duet

We are semi-retired after 40 years
under the moon's sway,
taking turns each month,
every month,
to cast an egg into waiting fronds,
a journey of risk into
a cave washed by a bloody sea.

We were thwarted by drugs,
rubber and copper.
We never gave up
our job to nurture
new life, bathe it deep,
watch it grow, kick.
We delivered.

Senescence loomed. We flung
out ova. Recklessness led
to a double triumph,
our final duet.
Now we relax, only
called on to sing when
our body recalls her animal self.

Mostly we sleep, grateful
to lie in our ligament
hammocks. Our
lunar dreams replay
those tidal surges, the work
we did giving rhythm and
shape to her fertile being.

Dr Pozzi

(Response to John Singer Sargent's 1881 portrait,
'Dr Samuel Jean Pozzi at Home'.)

His fingers clasp the collar
of his red velvet gown, rest
over the loosened cord.

Black hair, trimmed beard
his eyes reflect the light.
The draped curtain is opulent.

He is poised, secure in
his beauty, his gaze leaning
out of the frame. He invites

attention from admirers
who want to touch
his cloak, his slippered foot.

Women felt safe in his hands.
None of their husbands'
grunting and battering.

Dr Pozzi was gentle, understood.
He healed their unseen corners.
Comforted.

Later, years later, he lay
crumpled on the stone floor,
shot four times in the stomach.

He asked to be buried
clothed, wounds hidden
beneath his blue serge uniform.

Repeat Prescription

I want to prescribe panaceas
for teetering marriages,
for kids that disappoint.

I want to find spells
in my pharmacopoeia
to soothe the bruises
of pain and loss.

I want to give holidays
to those slaves whose
parents last forever,
forgetting themselves,
forgetting their children.

Every ten minutes
a patient leaves
gripping a script
for plasters,
pills, placebos –
I didn't want to sign.

Care

only for yourself and
the black dog, until you
grow heavy and dull.
Sink into water, mud,
hold your breath.
Slump inside, ban the sun,
talk to no one.

Forget the warmth of the body,
the embrace of others,
the lick of light on your skin,
in case you remember
how narcissi push through
white layers of frozen snow,
quiet on the curving hills,
as the days lengthen.

It Starts with a Fit

it starts with a fit out of the blue
you can't remember how or why
you're shocked it's happening to you

you're sure it's stress too much to do
you plan to cut down to really try
it starts with a fit out of the blue

you lose some words repeat a few
you grin and laugh I want to cry.
we're shocked it's happening to you

the scan confirms what we guessed is true
it doesn't explain how or why
it starts with a fit out of the blue

you're lost not sure what you should do
you search for answers in the sky
I'm shocked it's happening to you

you change from a man I loved and knew
to someone who seems like a passer-by
it starts with a fit out of the blue
you've stopped being shocked it's happening to you

Ode

Oh do not wonder at the joy with which we view the stool.
To ask about its many forms should be the surgeon's rule.
Without a blush our patients learn it's admirable to say
I've been just once, or not at all, or seven times today.
We need to know the quantity, the quality and size,
the colour, shape and odour, if they sink or if they rise.
Is there mucus, blood or slime? Are they black, dark brown or pale?
In every patient's motion hangs a fascinating tale.
The clues are diagnostic in the young and very old,
each individual product worth its weight in gold
So do not turn your nose up when we gaze into the loo,
a mass of information is revealed within each poo.

Consultation

You've got a terrible sore throat and streaming nose.
Sounds like a cold
And you're burning up. Feeling shivery.
Yes … well … you have got a slight fever
You've never felt this poorly.
That's not what your notes imply
And you've had it three whole days!
Do you know how long the average cold lasts?
You've got to get better soon.
I wish you would
Because you're going on holiday at the weekend.
Lucky for some …
So you thought you'd better pop in.
As an urgent appointment?
To make sure it wasn't going onto your chest.
Oh come on … you're not even coughing
In case you need some antibiotics.
No you don't
To prevent you getting pneumonia.
It's only a cold …
So what would I suggest …
Paracetamol
Is that all? No medicine?
And honey and lemon and fluids
But you feel really ill and exhausted.
More honey and lemon and fluids
And your chest hurts in the middle.
Steam inhalations and regular paracetamol
You don't know why you bothered coming.
Search me
You're surprised I'm not going to give you anything.
I'm not
Dr L. always gave you Amoxil … which always works.
Dr L. took the easy way out
If it gets worse, you'll blame me.

You'll be back.
I know …

Why I Should Stop Work

You are fat.
I don't care.
You don't care.
Let's talk about something else.
The weather? Your children?
No, not your children.
They are fat too.
I don't care.
You care a little.

This is the point at which
I should try and make you realise
you are going to die
before you have
finished living.
In fact, you may die
before you have
properly started.

You still don't care.
I don't much.

You eat.
I despair.
I did care.
You might have cared once.
But now you are fat,
you don't care
at all.

That makes it difficult
for me to care,
too.

Impact

drifting in a black ocean
          your heart leaves a trace
                    each breath sighs and clicks

five weeks later you emerge
          unable to speak
                    you are missing

parts
     of
       you

one limb is a ghost
          your guts have moved
                    out

memory is a white wall
          built of stories
                    told to you

you hold a hand,
          it might be yours
                    theirs

there are angels
          near the bed
                    faces covered in prayers

they say
          you are lucky
                    to be here

Examination

When you give me your map,
creased and scarred with use,
I run my hands over its contours
searching for landmarks I know:

the sternal notch, McBurney's point.
I don't want to trip on crags
or pebbles lying in valleys where
I'd expect to find sand.

My hands journey in places
only a lover might touch.
We smile with relief when
it's over. You get dressed.

I drive home in sudden snow,
flurries that change the shape
of everything. There'll be
black ice in the morning.

I ask you to make another appointment.

Acknowledgements

Many thanks to all the tutors and students on the MPhil in Writing course at the University of South Wales 2015-2017 who gave me helpful feedback on several of the poems that appear in this pamphlet.

Thanks also to the Poetry School for two excellent online courses that made me experiment with new subjects and forms of poetry.

I am also very grateful to the members of Leeds Writers Circle for their useful comments and support.

Differential was Highly Commended and published in the Hippocrates Prize Anthology 2016. *Six Week Check* won joint 3rd prize in the Hippocrates Prize for Poetry and Medicine 2018 and appeared in the Hippocrates Prize Anthology 2018. *Eye to Eye* was published under the title *Retina* in Strix 2 in 2017 and *Clinical Trials* appeared in Strix 3 in 2018.